ANXIETY IN MOSAIC

T0065486

NGOLLE-METUGE

Langaa Research & Publishing CIG
Mankon, Bamenda

Publisher:
Langaa RPCIG
Langaa Research & Publishing Common Initiative Group
P.O. Box 902 Mankon
Bamenda
North West Region
Cameroon
Langaagrp@gmail.com
www.langaa-rpcig.net

Distributed outside N. America by African Books Collective
orders@africanbookscollective.com
www.africanbookcollective.com

Distributed in N. America by Michigan State University Press
msupress@msu.edu
www.msupress.msu.edu

ISBN: 9956-578-14-2

DEDICATION

To Bate Besong

Fallen though, in this people's war
You never left your gun un-bequeathed, O soldier!

Table of Content

INTRODUCTION

Anxiety In Mosaic consists of a long poem; "Under The Prawn's Carapace" and a several shorter poems. These latter are grouped under a number of thematic sub-headings. Rich in its diversity of subject matter as well as in its philosophical decrying of certain insidious global social ills, the volume encapsulates socio-economic, governmental, historical, religio-moral, environmental and gender or feminist issues. In this vein therefore, concerns of personal bearing to the poet, the predominant ills that ravage a nation, the sinister notions that characterize the history of an entire continent as well as those that humanity as a whole face are all thrown in the mix of the numerous worrying issues raised in this seemingly compendious work of art to which there certainly couldn't have been a more befitting title. Otherwise put, the volume's concerns span realms which not only bear on the person of the poet but include nation, continent and the entire world. The long poem is essentially the bludgeoning, in lament, of a society in the process of being savaged to socio-economic and political rubble by the wanton, unbridled practice of esurience and human material surfeit.

Language is employed in a particularly volatile manner to tell, so very despairingly, of a system in ruinous hopelessness and deprivation. But a last, even in the midst of such hopelessness, there is the lurking possibility, nevertheless, of salvation for the system; a salvation whose attainment could be made less troublesome by the adoption of altruistic and, most especially, divinely-inspired ways.

N.M

PSYCHO-INSOMNIAC
Empathy in short circuits
(The prelude)

Whoever resides
Like a demon inside of me
And entwines
Like a creeper around my beauteous mind –
Choking off my sanity
And nourishing off
What little happiness
There is left in me –
Could never fathom still
What nameless cares
Waste me down
From inside the very depths
Of my marrow bones

Whoever liquefies into blood
To flow, transfused
Through my veins, partaking
In the beating of my heart
Shall never know still
What caustic fears and hopes
Seethe under my skin
Burning me thin,
What sundry hookworm anxieties
Have stuck unto my psyche's guts,
Eating me lean

Whoever sublimates
From human into ether
Dissolving into the mind
To become one with the psyche

Could never fathom still
What matchete*d* ponderings
Slaughter sleep
Down in my eyes

For I know
Even as I write
No matter how hard I try
Adjectives alone can't duplicate for real, for you
My pangs of this world; all the empathy, flowing
But in short circuits...
And you won't know exactly still –
From these second hand excruciations only –
The manner of drab in which is hued my pain, and the
death
Of which I die…

For who, but he that cries
Can himself tell
Of tears shed in the rain?
The falling showers
Drenching every eye
Of every face

ECO-DEVILRY

BURNED TO SADNESS

In the sun a bush burns
Down to sadness
A black rapacity moves up in a billowy gait
For all to see
The favourite pastime of men

The grazing bull nearby
Cowers away in a hundred moos
Two egrets cringe toward the ominous sky;
Home of the winged marooned

I drink from tears
That fall down the eyes of homeless birds
As underneath the sticks and stones of alarmed youth
The shimmering black snake
Crawls for refuge

In posh houses founded on graft
They drink
The blood in a decanter that passes for wine;
Them; vampyric bane of creation
And dance to the dirge-cries
Of menaced cormorants, played back
For the listening and dancing displeasure
Of my wearied soul

Morning comes
To show me the night's dewy tears, upon
The green grass of home turned brown;
The night's dewy tears, shed
For these iniquitous things

SINCE GREEN BECAME MY FAVOURITE COLOUR

Since green became my favourite colour
And greed smacked of their favourite odour
My heart has made the acquaintance
Of rubber plantations, which, for nothing but a farthing
Did belabour my father's hands
And out of which was made
The tyres of the car that leaves – on the asphalt,
A millipede squashed to pulp

Since green became my favourite colour
And greed smacked of their favourite odour
Midnight has tabled – a thousand times before my ears –
The chirped-out grievances of discontented cicadas

My heart has made the acquaintance
Of rubber plantations, which, for nothing but a white
franc
Did belabour my mother's hands
And out of which was made
The old pair of Wellington boots that now remind me
Of blind wayfaring long ago
And the crunch of a horned beetle underneath its soles

Since green became my favourite colour
And greed smacked of their favourite odour
I've made out, from afar,
The slaughter of *obeches** in the keen snarl of chainsaws
Spilling – on leaves and blades of grass –
Sawdust blood of cream white hue

Since green became my favourite colour…

* kind of tropical hardwood tree used in making furniture

LITTLE YEVGENY

Upon viewing a TV documentary on Chernobyl and its likes.
The very likelihood of their recurrence.

Of sorrow, once, I died
For little Yevgeny
Born into 'ego-lunacy';
One more son
Of that soil, watered
By hemlock rivers

On pity, once, I surfeited
Dying
For little Yevgeny, walking-a-wobble
His wasteland home of corrosive breezes

Rather the sordidness I see here;
This indigence in my blood of ebony
Than a life like little Yevgeny's

For a blond hair'd lad, once, I died
For little Yevgeny, his summers
Made of cyanide noons; the tender-marrowed prey
Of mutant potatoes from that subterranean lair
Of arsenic peat; ratsbane-tubers
For Slavic mandibles; vampire-staple
Chewing to chaff
His toddler's brain

Tell me, how many penultimate Armaggedons —

Till the end of sunshine – stand
At the Baltic's backyard?
How many little Yevgenys more
For a lesson to learn?
Better this melanin stigma of mine;
This dark brand upon my whole self
Than a lot
Like little Yevgeny's

ECO-DEVILRY

Into my slumber
Slowly creeps a nightmare: eco-devilry
Wherein these long-throats of krakens of men
Swallow down to Armageddon
The leafed things of this world

Nightmare
Wherein goodwill, like bread,
Bakes into hard, crispy selfishness
Down in the oven-days of this vexed sun
That balances – at noontide upon my head –
A zillion-degree-Celsius load of suffering

What refuge then, O! poor polar pal,
Would be that ice-roofed home of yours
Stilted
On quicksnow ?

TO SHED A GREEN TEAR

To shed a green tear…

To weep
For these last of secretary birds on the run
Flying away never to return
And for presidents yet unborn, who shall behold –
But in the extant photos of their crimson days in office –
The winged evanescence

To shed a green tear…

To cry
For the foul breath wafted in the sun
From lake Beri's miasma yawn,
For her watery bowels, still hurting
From industrial food poisoning

To shed a green tear…

To wail
For that restless chatter of gibbons
Petering out of the tree tops of the east
For contrast with the Buddhist mind
No more an example shall it constitute;
No more of it shall we hear

To shed a green tear…

To weep, aghast
At those billowing rockets of black and white, fired
From Uncle Sam's chimneys, and going to make
Of Julys and Septembers, the incinerators wherein

Our days shall, to cinders, come

To shed a green tear…

I WEEP

For dynamited gold mines agape with dereliction, lying
Like hollowed-out trunks of *iroko*,
Smelling like burnt-out caves
I weep

For the distant cries I hear
Of devoured wilds
Down in the deep un-purged bowels of westerly cupidity
I weep

For ugl*ified* reefs of coral
That wail in the azure bosom of lady Atlantic,
For that beauty, lost, of mermaids;
That comeliness, raped
By the sewage-dross from gluttonous machines
I weep

For those vitals,
Forever lost
Where pillaged things go;
For that which the sun shall neither retrieve for me
Nor men shall ever regain

For these gelded grounds;
The menopausal womb of greed-haggard Africa
I weep…
For that which the moon shall never again

Make fecund;
That which haunt me still
From nightmares of long ago

HIGH HEAVEN

High heaven, to which reeks
A nation's faeces; the churned undigested pilferages
Shat out via anuses of greed

High heaven, to which smack
These contaminants of graft, farted
From the champagne*ous* bulges
Of pressurised-can stomachs

Forgive us the blasphemy

High heaven, where go these whiffs
Of festering terribleness, wafted
From the street corners of thrash can-cities

And to which rise
These *Babelian* heights
Of disposed assorted dross;
The Himalayan dustbins of downtowns

Forgive us the desecration

HORRID PROPENSITY

MIRROR IMAGE

Within this spherical mirror image, distorted
By many-a-billion horned desires on two legs
There is the pigsty-beauty
Of faces I see, their laughter of topaz, lost
In the mirage of moneyed trifles, their souls
Of lust-dried mud, crumbling
All day long
And their hearts of iron, rusting
All night long, from
Those mere alluring putrescibles of carnal land

Light up – O! Guide with the torch
Of a zillion suns – this tenebrous way;
Lead us sightless ones
Where shines your moon of indigo blue

HERE SPRAWLS THE GREAT SAHARA

Here sprawls the great Sahara;
One of its kind
Yet belittled by the vaster wildernesses of men's vicious
minds.
I'm going blind

Over there stands mighty Everest
Yet dwarfed by mightier mountains of greed and phobia
complexes.
My mind perplexes

Every now and then is the sound of the Great Trumpet
Yet drowned by calls of darkness even louder

Than a thousand peals of thunder
Rumbling through endless stormy nights.
These obscure cataclysmic times leave me trembling with
wonder

And here and there
Is goodwill and peace bedevilled,
Lying
In ashen uselessness in the crematoria of evil.

That these vain trespasses of mere mortals
Could ug*lify* the wondrous natural comeliness of mother
earth so divine
Bewilders my very soul
And makes my blood run cold

But until the last but one drop of Atlantic waters
Has drenched all but a grain of Saharan sands,
In scalding pools of tears we shall forever stand

BURNING DUMB WITNESS

Between July leaves fresh and green
Penetrates a shower of rays;
I bathe in your sun spray.

Weave me a gilded morning
That in the stillness of this place
I may sit and listen
To the oral tales of your secrets
Muted in golden shafts
Telling
Of unspeakable mountain piles

Of shrouded indignities that burn
In the blaze of your timeless memory
Down to the ashes of forgiveness divine

Of skulls and the crushed bones of innocents
Strewn in the darkest grottoes of politics
Of trillion zillion tons of blasphemy, hurled
At you – since the day your eyelid melted away –
From warped scriptures, mangled creeds
And capsized dogmas

And of swindling gluttons who grope
In the dark of benighted lands
Lugging pilferages from coffers and vaults

Coruscating orb Divine
Sitting decently on high,
Unblinking omniscient spy (of all good and all
machinations)
You who uncovers the nooks and crannies of falsehood
To the daylight jeer of truth
Vouchsafe me that impossible knowledge
Of the things you see
But of which you utter not a word,
Of how much nuclear greed per heart per nation
There is down here
And how many phobic heights more to ascend
Before the end of days

Eyeball of gold fire
You burning dumb witness
To age old truths and numberless un-divulged things

Take this proffered hand reaching out for you

And lead me far far away into your omniscience,
Into your eternity and into that wondrous power
Which only a man's bosom friend is privy to
That, as you slowly sail
Across this overhead sea of grey,
I may behold you at midday without squinting
Without going blind.

BEASTS

In this animal kingdom
Here, where jackals eat jackals
And cub devours mother hyena,
On full stomachs
Predators prowl still the jungle
For prey

In this animal kingdom
Here, where giant tapeworms of insatiability
Reside deep down the desires of beasts
And appetites run wilder
Than wild boars in dense wilds,
A hunter heads home
Bleeding from a damaged conscience, gun in hand
And his own brother man
Slung over his shoulder:
Quarry for the long-throated

In this animal kingdom
Here, where some self-proclaimed kings of beasts
Rival one another
Just to be entitled

To that great dishonour of most supreme savage under
the sun,
A covetous and noisy bald eagle
Sits atop sky-scraping sequoias, trusting in God
And wondering how many sunsets more to go
Before losing its crown
To become just a face in the crowd.

In this animal kingdom…
This animal kingdom
Of nations

THE LOST'S PRAYER

Our dollar
Which art of the Devil
Hollowed be thy name, thy *slavedom* come
Thy ill be done on Nooremac as it is in Erebus
Give us each day our daily gripes
And deceive US All stupid asses
As we believe in dross to amass
Around us
And lure us more into damnation
As thy believers lust for evil

For thine is this *skindom*
The power for the gory
Forever but never,
Amen

OF WIDOWS AND MAIDENS

THE PIANIST OF LIBREVILLE

With chords as of shrieks
Wrung out of a keyboard tormented by black fingers
In Libreville a pianist told
Of her woe

Chords like a hand
Raised the curtain
And I saw what heavy rains fell
Inside a heart

Chords shaped like truth
Bared before me; my eyes of sympathy
The corners of a mind
Nibbled away by a rodent-privation

Chords as of a glow in a dark room
By which I saw
The blood under the bolted door
Flowing from a stabbed heart

From a keyboard
Tormented by black fingers
In Libreville a pianist told
Of her woe…
The pain through which
Her sisters go

HYMENS

When hymens were doors; doors of iron
One trespass only
Was the key
To a dinning room
Where they eat
With spoons and forks of blood

When hymens stood
Taller than castle gates
Just a trespass away
Lay the heavenly haven
Where warm summers never end

When hymens stood
More imposing
Than fortress towers
It was through them
That men traversed
Into countries sometimes more populous
Than great China
With densities of up to seven earthlings
Per square foot
Of ante-natal land

It was through hymens
As tall as heaven's gate
That noble Martin
Exited
Into the sunshine

Who desecrated hymens then
The great object of my honour?

OF WIDOWS AND MAIDENS

For you whose lot
Is a lot dingier and muddier than mine
I pray
That from your divine heights of fecundity
Yet truer Kings and Wilberforces
May see the light of day

Of widows and maidens; the mere ribbed afterthought
of the Creator,
I tell my tale.
Under which shelter of water
Have you been taking cover
Since these acid rains directed at you
Began to fall?

But as long as life survives
Wrapped in the cocoon of eternity
Who shall ever rid you of your nature's native beliefs?
You; the arable land of ungrateful macho farmers
For even in the passing away of history;
That oral tale of truth, I shall forever be
Your only child
I shall be like America
Never forgetting
The taste of black amniotic fluid
In which she bathed in pre-natal days
In the womb of pregnant mother Africa

So may those shackles all over you
Melt further down
Further down beyond today's anklets and bangles and
necklaces

Till, like a smile, you go hanging
Upon the lips of Time

Nurture with utmost care, O! you niggers of gender,
Your Lincolns and Mandelas;
Those fragile lilies and magnolias that sprout
Upon the volcanic soils
Of your raging quest

THE SECRET OF POOR LITTLE SYLVIA

No wreath, no bed
He lay there
Frowning
At his turn to sleep
The last slumber of men

And no one knew why
Of all the eyes that looked on
None but poor little Sylvia's
Streamed with tears

Out in the courtyard – where night
Was just starting to pull,
Over the day's dusky face,
It's dark shroud – there was
The talk in whispers that went by,
Very like tiny whistling breezes among the dusk-covered
leaves –
Of the unbreakable canker of steel
That had sealed once and for all, the eyes
Of he who lay there, frowning
At his turn to sleep

The last slumber of men

And no one knew why
Poor little Sylvia cried so hard
At the talk in whispers that went by
Very like tiny whistling breezes

No tear, no bier
He lay there
Smoke-dried human game,
Lean ribbed ghastliness
Mummified…
Into the iceman's wholesomeness

And out in the yard
Where the owl's hooting monotone
Made a long sonorous gash on the evening's torso,
They pronounced – in whispers that went by very like
Tiny whistling breezes – inverted eulogies
For he who loved to lie on others; he
On whom earth shall now love to lie

And no one knew why
Of all the eyes that looked on
None but poor little Sylvia's
Streamed with tears as he lay there
In lifeless dishonour to all mankind
No dirge no homage, his ribs
Laughing out to all, his lips
Parting away disgruntled, setting forth their fellow teeth;
The clenched malevolence,
For all to see

And out in the yard

The talk in whispers went by – very like
Tiny whistling breezes amongst the dusk-covered leaves
–
That it could be poor little Sylvia cried, carrying simply
In her heart, a teenager's mere fondness
For he who lay there, frowning
At his turn to sleep
The last slumber of men

But no one knew…
No one knew
Poor little Sylvia's secret rapist
Had placed in her tender little heart and soul
The fear of the devil
And on she wept, poor little Sylvia
Not knowing
That some anti-retroviral day this day
She shall lie there…
Smiling rather
At her own turn to sleep
The last slumber of men

FENCE*
Amazon Mama

Wooden dilapidations of drab;
The tottering, straw-roofed homes
Tilt over gutters of long-standing slime;
Sad enemies of the nostrils

Close by
A bare skinny lad in greasy rags
Plays with his crown corks

As inside the suffocation of their sultry shack
His Amazon mama groans at excruciating titillations
Of the manhood.
The long-tortured bed in its turn
Grumbles out loud at the strain of every move

Upon creaking hinges
The poor aged door swings open
Ah! Good morning in the burning afternoon
But he sneaks out bashfully, buttoning up away
Feeling bad

Outstretched hands then fling far
Water from a bucket: after-wash of the hurriedly cleaned
womanhood
Whose tiny splashes catch the gutter lads at their play.
The man on the road spits out a sigh

In an earth-mound verandah
Sits her on her low stool, tarrying the next caller
Her gaze follows the passer by
The length of the street

To her; his Amazon mama
And to him; her famish-eyed 'bastard'
Does daily bread fall thus
From skies of sweat
Or offered
By the base hands
Of ignominy?

I wonder
*A neighbourhood. K-Town

29

OF BLOOD...
Fadimatou's Question

There are lands and lands that bleed
From the muzzle and bomb gashes of greed
Their red red rivers
Taking their rise
From battlefields

There is the civil gore
In which is drenched
Those homelands that have attempted suicide
To hang down by the nooses
Of rapacity's tail
Longer
Than the gibbon's

There is the blood too
That rained cats and dogs
Down from Rwanda's skies
Done
In those crimson days of the year of their lord

And pure Aryan blood there was
That once stank
Of sins that brought to the eyes
Of even the utmost gumption,
Dark dark tears of horror

And that too
From the slit throats of four-legged ones
Washed
In vain
Down the drains

Of gluttony's abattoir
Are they – boars of men whose hands
These kinds of bloodshed have stained –
Any less unclean
Than us; breasted souls whose period comes
Only
Divinely
Through no fault of ours?

MOTHER OF MEN

THIS NAME

With what disinfectant
Mixed with the waters of the Nile
Shall I cleanse this name; this name
Contaminated by the halitosis
Of mouths that utter it in disdain; this name
Trampled upon in the stampede of defamations, lying
In centuries long, of coma?

In what poetic forge
Shall I straighten this name, fashioned
After a question mark; this name
Mangled out of shape in its head-on collision with
A trailer*ful* of frozen epithets?

In what blast furnace – fired
By a thousand and one degree Celsius of verse power –
Shall I remake this name; I –
This smith with a pen?

In which detergent-silted ocean
Shall I – washer man-poet, immerse this silken name;
This silken name, stained
By soiling fingers; the soiling fingers
Of opinions, sired
By prejudice; this name inscribed in the Sahara,
Half-defaced by sieving western winds that go by
Whispering of globalisation?

And I – washer man-poet, shall sit
On a kitchen stool by the Niger's meanders
To wash clean this name; this name
Dirtied

With the smear of propagandist grease; this name
Spotted here and there with the rusty marks
Of libellous stains

POBRE MADRE *

Pobre madre, mi pobre madre
Intrepid tigress moves
Toward death from which
The world runs away helter-skelter

Still, no perturbations rock
The emotions of your being
You whom indigence has raped and battered
These several tenebrous decades gone by

Pobre madre, mi pobre madre
Lone, dry-eyed amazon, tranquil
Amid these many crying faces I see

Your pretty face
Is one on which smiles
Usurp the place of tears
Even as spiky years
Flagellate to the soul

Pobre madre, mi pobre madre
Stillness…
Unmoved
In this very vortex of transcience
Elephantine anvil
Standing in the whirlwind

May heaven succour you!
Lying marooned in this wilderness of flinty times
For when slavery begets immortality, O *pobre madre*!
Who can plot with success, your demise?
You who sweated centuries in the sun,
Remaining poor
Just to give others their bulging purses
Of today

* Spanish for *poor mother*
* *Poor mother, my poor mother*

LOVE POEM

Sitting on a Saharan dune
My love's heart breaks of dearth
In my wildest dream, wilder
Than elephant grass
I have borrowed the sweet voice
Of many-a-songbird
To sing her a love song of all that, in vanity's hands –
Does lie

In my fervent wish, dreamier
Than wishful thinking
I have borrowed the humming voice
Of many-a-distant waterfall
To mend – with a ballad on illusion –
My love's broken heart of indigence

Parch-mouthed, my darling awaits me
Sitting on the Namib's doorstep
And in my profoundest longings, more profound

Than a hundred rift valleys,
I have borrowed the mellifluous voice of many-a-river
To sing her a ballad on illusion;
A ballad of hope

So lend me your silent voices, O many-a-palm grove!
That under tonight's blessed moon
I may stand outside her window
And gently gently serenade my love awake from her
sleep;
Her nightmarish slumber of privation

TRUEST MOTHER

You, from whose inexhaustible breasts
Babies and foster-children
From distant and enemy lands
Have suckled generously to their fill,
You are the truest mother of men

You, who only smile,
At the ingratitude of grown up nations
Which you rocked to sleep on your ancient lap
When they were babies,
You are the truest mother of men

Today, that umbilical cord
From you to all your children; nations big and small
Cannot be severed with such
A blunt-edged epithet
As *Dark Continent*

And tomorrow, truest mother…!

As you go about your chores of motherhood,
Keep strapped, upon your aged back,
With those very loins of kindness,
Your great, great grand children

ALIEN CULPABILITY

SUCCOUR

How many numberless miles
Of this barefooted mad rush
Over the shards of shattered vitreous hearts
Must I cover
Before the succour of the woollen road?

How many trillion times against walls
Must I bump and bump
And gropings to and fro must I make
Before it dawns here
In my dark cell
Of this prison
Round and round the sun?

And thinking
Of those savage days, when,
With an old colonial piece of iron, now rusted
They pulled my eyeballs
Out of their sockets
And how I've since stolen Europe's blue eyes
To use to shed my pitch black tears of Africa

How many numberless crumbs and crumbs
Of bread must I live on
Over this path to endless laughter
Before the succour
Of my destination's streets paved with gold ?

MORATORIUM

Toil in the sun
Sweat from my brow
Runs down the black of my face
And away it goes
Like a river that flows
Paying off the debt owed you
For your air that I breathe and my gold you stole
Paying…
Not in your dollars
But in crumbs, gleaned
From the abject*est* corner of indigence

Pain in the heat
Sweat from my brothers' brows
Runs down the black of their faces
And away it goes
Like streams that flow
Paying off all that is due you
For your sunlight which they get;
For your war in which they fought and died
That you may live in peace
Paying…
All that is due you
Not in your euros
But in scrapings from the most sordid side
Of poverty

Who shall grant them a lasting moratorium; these
Coarse palms of our hands?

Who shall oblige us with the longest sleep ever;
The last slumber of men?

FIGHT AGAINST POVERTY

When, for long-throats diseased with Gallic thirst
They stopper in champagne bottles my pipe-borne sweat
How much of a matador can I be
Against this horned penury that charges at me
Down this arena, thronged
By aristocratic pro-bull spectators?

When the drains still lie, unblocked
That empty into the storage tanks of Switzerland
How well can I take up cudgels
Against this snarling and spiky-tailed privation
Going berserk at me?

And when, in this teeming market place,
Men of goodwill
And thieves with greed-spangled intent
Pick even these empty pockets of mine
Then, for a ghost purpose, I rise
To slay this indigence-mouthed ugliness;
This hunger-winged vampire bat
That nightly sticks cold fangs
Into my scrawny neck

EVEN OUT

A cashew nut tree
Planted in Timbuktu
Grew above the clouds
And over the Atlantic
Fruiting in distant lands

And I shall cry
Over woes insubmersible in booze;
Expert swimmers
That catch up with me
Again and again
Across a Mississippi of frothing alcohol

And I shall cry
Till I windsurf at the beach of Malibu
On a piece of broken palm nut shell

Cry,
Till I slalom at Christmas
On skis of coconut shell, gliding
Over snows amid the leftovers
Of New York's conifers

An acacia tree
Planted in Kaniaga
Grew past the Sahara
Branching out over the Mediterranean
To flower in faraway lands

And I shall wail
Over clinging troubles refusing to be shaken off
Even in the violent moves
To beats of *coupé–decalé*
I shall wail
Over a cashew nut tree rooted in Timbuktu,
Its foliage above the snow;
I shall wail
Till I sail
In a boat of hollowed-out cola nut
Over a Thames of foaming palm wine

CROCODILE FRIEND

Last week
A crocodile friend of mine arrived, business-like.
He trailed a luggage full of shackles
In which, bound, he took me away
Across the deep blue sea

Three days ago
My crocodile friend came back,
Cassock draped over his rotting torso,
Wreaking havoc like a tornado;
Splitting in two the wooden effigies
In my sacred shrines

Then just the other day
My crocodile friend returned, yet unsatisfied
Usurping my throne of iroko,
Reigning over me
And holding between his lips, like a drinking straw,
The tip of my severed artery

Now with his long-throat and hands
My crocodile friend is here again
Diddling me at the market place of the world.
This heinous crime of today
I will, however, forgive
For it is only money
And money swindled
Can always be repaid
But as for my manhood on which he trampled
That, I shall never forget
For before history's unblinking eyes
Dignity, once lost, is hard to regain

Hard to regain
My crocodile friend

GAME

Too much talking
This Tuesday morning
On air

I read between the radio's lines
What's been granted
By fiscal heaven:
Stained quarter on a gilded string:
Poisoned penny
Shall drop from
The International Manipulations Firmament
Into the mendicant's cupped hands:
Completion point

In this game of cheat-belly;
Blackjack at WTO;
Casino
Where affluent but partial gamblers
Skilfully deal the cards of trade;
Their minds
Set
Like that
Of the hissing tongue-flicker in the Garden of Eden

Where the fraternity, the equality and the justice…
Where the fair play
When black privation confronts white surfeit
At monopoly?

Globalisation performs at the circus.
Against my will I shall be the rapt spectator
While the juggler wins
And the magician carries the day
Far from me
Like an oddment
Swept away by rainwater

THE COMING OF SCARLET DAYS

In witness I stand
Like a deity;
Guest of honour at the christening of moments;
The sunny moments of fleeting eras
And I grant you
These moments go
By a western name;
These moments shown here
Right here…
On the charted pedigree of Time

In witness I stand
Like a goddess;
Guest of honour at the naming ceremony of days;
The rainy days of rushing epochs
And I warrant you
These days right here
Are called Washington;
These days shown here,
Right here…
On the charted pedigree of Time

But there, on the horizon of eternity's restlessness
There, where the sea meets skies
At once cloudy and fair
I see them slowly come; the scarlet days of
The turning of tides,
Days with the freshness of hatchlings;
Fresh scarlet days
Soon to be shown…
There, somewhere
On the uncharted pedigree of Time
I see them slowly come:
Fresh scarlet days
Answering to names
Stranger than western
Stranger than Washington

MIGRANT, LEARNER OR QUISLING...?

AT FEAR'S END
For The Winter's Advent

Such inevitable things
As summer's golden goodbye
Which breaks Europe's hearts of china
Are now the eternal waters
That quench my flaming thirst

In such a silence
When nothing stirs but the somersault
Of these sunset-coloured leaves
Which could well have been plucked
By a baby's breath
To land here at my stranded feet, so noiselessly
That I recall how so oblivious I had been
Of things that fall without a thud

And at such a Finnish place,
Here, where marooning January's head
Already comes to a faint view
Over yellow November's horizon,
In dread I stand no more
At this foreboding
Of yet another miserable white nights and days
When a sad-eyed economic migrant
Would have been waiting
To stand aggrieved at his window
Watching the fall of snow flakes
And holding again in his freezing mind,
But in vain,
That sunshine on ebony faces
That had gone slipping through his fingers

Such inevitable things…
Are now the eternal waters that quench
My blazing thirst;
The lesson by which I now grow

Tampere, Finland. Nov. 1999

EL DORADO

I trod the path to a wildest dream
There…
To catch a shadow
Via times as those, when
The child in me did make the acquaintance
Of Finnish days
Scowling at him through bleakness-rimed spectacles

Times,
When I longed to scuttle, rat-like
Across icy meadows
My frostbitten head to rest
Upon the pillow-afternoons of home

Over the plains of delusion
And down to El Dorado
I rode my hopes
Through times
Such as those when
February days donned their grey caps
At a miserable angle

Times,
When I walked, Christ-like

Over wildernesses of cold
By the sun's fireplace to sit
And feel frozen blood melt down in porous veins

THE HAND

Upon the shrine of Heaven
Barefoot I stand
Holding out in offering, this page;
My penned gratitude
For those shrouded truths
Vouchsafed me in a flash
Of lightening more lasting
Than a leap year,
The eyes that looked with pity upon me; my tribulations
And the hand that – with a duster –
Did wipe off my soul
The darkness thereon scribbled in charcoal gloom;
The hand that buoyed me up
In the tenebrous tides of furious seas,
Tossing me ashore all the way
And the hand that moved home
My stranded feet – me, this quisling of a runaway calibre
–
Guiding down the snowy road
Their faltering steps.
The hand that rescued –
From the cold wilderness of strange-looking Februarys –
This greed-tossed
And once marooned soul

BUSHFALLER

Of that accursed tree
Which grows upside-down
And away from the sun,
Mortification, not pride
Is what I feel
To be a leaf; a leaf
Of that accursed tree

Of that soil
Which lies, profaned
By the percolation of urinary vitriol
Pissed out via cancerous cunts and penises,
Humiliated, not proud
Is how it feels
To be a son; a son
Of that soil
Which lies, profaned…

But in that dark middle of nowhere;
That sun*less* triangular limbo
Where minds grow
Against all odds
Like giants into dwarfs

Privation,
And not this ostrogothic denigration
I should have chosen, nonetheless:
The adversary to face, fighting
Back to back with the valorous
Back to back with the conscious

Malversation,
And not this blond marginalisation
I should have chosen, nonetheless:
The bull to take by the horns, standing
On the side of the patriots
On the side of the conscious

Helsinki, Finland. July 2001

UNDER THE PRAWN'S CARAPACE

In this literary wail
From the sizzling, malversational excruciation
Of iron-brand wrongs done to man,
A chagrined biro
Sheds its ink-tears verselessly on paper

Lamentation

I

Watery stool in the bowl
Spiced with salt and pepper
Passes for *achu* soup
And on diarrhoeic days like these
Anal minds of state
Defecate their ego-faeces
In the mouths of us accursed simpletons
While urine from the royal bladder
Of Paul the First; king in despoliation,
Has drenched the people to the soul

In the offing, I see the times
Turned inside out: afternoon starts the day,
Then midnight, followed by dusk
Till the rain falls
From the earth to the sky

I am the omen of this 'upside-down ness'
I augur well for the sad tale
That shall come
To be told a few dark nights away from this day
That the entire chiefdom had committed suicide at dawn
Every tribesman and woman

Hanging down from the greed-noosed halter
What, for hell's sake, am I gibbering of?
Of slime and reek under the prawn's carapace;
Of you, kitchen waste from the household
Of oligarchic voraciousness,
And of me; the Anglophonic wretched
Of this earth of scathophagous politicking

And what's become of our sea breeze?
Dead-rat halitosis exhaled in my face
This late afternoon by the ocean's windy yawn
On a Tuesday as bleak as all the others
Since the oligarchic chieftain and his close collaborators
Began wasting from the rot of dementia

II
See me here, O kindred eyes of the betrayed!
Standing this high on the rostrum
Of a treason, higher
Than gaol walls, deadlier
Than death row - and hearken,
All ye ears that bleed from the jagged edges of keen
moans –
My own cry of lamentation, telling
Of black hands that strangle me between the lines
Of this literary blabber; a soul
Wronged by the surfeit of men

Here, where the winged cost of basic needs
Soar, like kites, to the skies
I sit, enfeebled
By purchasing weakness from the proboscis
Of governors, stuck down my neck

In nights of sleep
Without a single soul to see in my dream
Down to what Gomorrah
Leads this dirt road; this dirt road, watered
With the retch of inhuman beings –
Death's bequest for me, plied by hearses –
Up from this place of ice-cold faces
That stare at me from the dark, franc*less* black-outs
Of economic nights?

III
Morning exhales its breath of staleness in my face
On polling days covered with mildew.
In the blurred corner of noon
Darksome compatriots play the gubernatorial chess;
The dimly lit room
Of this casino of state where masked compatriots
Handle cards in gloved hands, seated
At the table of election-blackjack

To them goes a recompense
And to the rat mole-engineers who dug
The subway that links coffers and the pockets
Of trousers worn by their Excellencies.
I boycott, then, this ceremony
In honour of white-collar traitors,
Of medals and epaulettes for pilfering awardees
Under the three colours that have sworn to mother
rainbow
That they shall never again be the ones
To flutter high over a land that claims
It is one of glory

Here, where hearts carry mountainous desires
To satisfy hillock-sized needs,
Off my blood richly endowed, O! brother,
Lives this parliamentary *draculocracy*

And if only you knew
What astral cogitation
This righteousness that exalteth my nation brings me
Then you would understand
Why I pray, saying:
Flow over this mind, O meander of elixir
To wash the squalor off our souls!

IV
We goats whom greener pastures
Have shunned to damnation,
No choice have we but to bare our bodies
And brave this iron-brand economic hostage crisis
Red-heated in the privatisation furnace

What America to protect me
From this kamikaze of klepto*cracy*
When terrorists of cupidity strike,
Blowing down – to a rouble of destitution –
The trade centre of my world?

Of patriots and quislings (but of quislings more so)
Shall be said those things
Of which death alone knows how
To make men forgive
Yet forgetting not

So Nyobé, my Guevara!

And you, Likenye! Big brothers in arms:
You who trod fearlessly the decrepit hammocks over
black waters;
You who took over the chanting when our voices broke
In the middle of the long song, longer
Than ten thousand arduous symphonies, may your tears
flow –
From across the mountains of transcendence – into
mine,
For that land of promise whose worth, it is sung, no
tongue can tell
Yet auctioned for two farts and a belch in this
Endo-parasitic marketeering

Countless nightfalls
Have stood in blur between you and I
Since that day of cold blood, O soldiers of the people!
Still I hear, seeping through this steely dark,
The admonishing of your ethereal voices
To mean that
The pain from klepto-ethnocratic tyrannies
Is like the sizzling feel
Of slavish iron-branding on the scrotum
Imagine, sir!

V

With graft-ulcerated hearts they lay there;
Satyrs in this great saprophytic malversation.
It is said they died of ego-hypertension, when,
During a storm, and furious at being abused,
Greed struck thunder-like upon the land,
Shattering skulls and addling brains;
Tainting ventricles and perverting psyches

So in this nocturnal stretch of eternity
Like a million midnights rolled into one,
Dead I stand. Time,
When sarcophiles of gorgon-looking selves
Prey on carnal others

Me, O my countrymen!
Dissolved to ribs in penury-acid, prepared
By the defalcationist hands
Of political chemists gloved in good governance
 And if only you knew, O people!
What astral cogitation
This righteousness that exalteth my nation brings me
Then you would understand
Why I pray, saying:
Sympathy, sympathy O dark sky!
And cry me rains that cleanse dirtied consciences;
Bactericide of shower-tears
To disinfect these purulent hearts
That teem with the staphylococci of perversion

Festering minds, full
Of the thought-bacteria
That manifest into dead rat-stench-acts, posed
By hands that the rodent-gangrene of state
Has nibbled down to leprous proportions

Where the cudgel
To clobber to pulp and gore
Every limbless toad, stranded
In the downtown slime of this marshland?

VI

Unlike a tree in the thunderstorm
My humble abode rocks to seisms of anal plosion:
The harder they fart; the Pharisees of this Judea of mine
named after the prawn,
The smellier the air of pride I breathe
This Sabbath, the seventy-eighth day of June
When noble souls return from church, having sat
At pews nearest the altar; a million christian leagues
adrift from God;
The swine-necked, toad-stomached, Zaccheus-statured
communicants;
Consumers of the body and blood...
Of men

Clad in hypocrisy – the upper
Of their graft-soled shoes, made
Of the flesh of kin – discarded things they make of
prayers
As when the billionaire's wife
Begged God urgently for widowhood

Still I look in vain
For the world, lost again
Underneath a dung mountain of trespasses
Since that greatest of forgiveness at Calvary

VII

The hearts of all the king's men, so ego-bloated
They bursted at their seams
And before international eyes
They staged the sparrowhawk dance charade;
That governmental affectation, baptised

With avian water

But I tell you, O people!
To disenthrall your soul selves from this mesmerism of
foolery
Is to kill – with the catapult of incredulity –
That mocking bird

When the mind's touch
Shares this dead-leaf crispiness
Of which my most cherished dream has become,
Roasted dry by the edacious rays
Of our clime's summer sun, I pray – O Greatest
Phantom,
For detergent rains on this pungent corner of
humankind
Lost in delusion
Under the soles of Your glorious feet

Useless days like prayers without *Amens*
Have crumbled the building blocks
Of my dreams to castles in the air.
Inertia of rot has stilled me to desuetude
Since employers' heads
Began rolling at this great guillotine of *crise economique*
So what work to find
Here, where I've had as many *honours most respectfully...*
As to deplete the ink in a million ball-point pens,
Numbing to paralysis the hand that writes them?

VIII
In an endless sleep
Without a cockcrow to raise me from this death,

A black-suited, iron-teethed mammalian terribleness
Crunched the bones of its young

So what gulag for them; cannibalist criminals;
The decision-making destroyers of bright futures?

In an interminable night shunned by the dawn
A hideous thing with a hundred thousand mouths and
anuses
Lived off the entrails of clansmen

This genre of gulosity; the people's own neurosis
Is the syphilis that excavates a borehole
In the brain matter of my tribe's notables

And everywhere in a wasteland of rapacity
The crescendo of ululant laments
Reverberates over the ruins of our rectitude;
Sole ethical legacy of reverent forebears, which we –
The money-minded beatniks of our altruist ethos,
Have profaned with apostasy
Wondering stretches the mind to breaking point,
About how the pilfering fingers alone,
Of hearts that covet,
Could lay this far to waste
The lives of men

Talk of stenches, of eye and ear sores
And of crabs in their pubic hair

In this blackout of graft
How much longer
Shall my guiltless face hold on to its lustre
Before I begin to grope with you; wayfarers in

delinquency,
To that nameless of places where benighted
fatherlanders
Sing anthems to the dark?

I fly away;
Blind flight that lands me, still
In the esurient waters of this Erebus disgraced with
sun*less* days

Into what detergent for stained minds, O Creator of
Mwankum!
Shall we dip this soiled cloth of a conscience?

If only you knew
What death it is I die of, standing
In this stone's throw from the place of perdition,
Then you would understand why I pray, saying:
Only with inhuman feet may I walk again, O lord!
On ways milkier than any that man could ever dream of

IX
When greed is allergy, gotten
From contact with the slime of gangrene days
And the groundnut city's red-carpeted corridors
Are odorified by sixty seven whiffs of our reek of state,
How can my loud-mouthed biro
Not propagate this *kongossa*
Of constables I've seen
Cleaning themselves up with the national flag
After defecating in the republic's mouth?

How long must I stand

In the floodlights of indignity
For goings-on which make
For that brand of inspiration that flows
Into my imagination but in coprophagous bounds?

How long must I stand
In this glare of shame, looked at
With that condescension
In western eyes that peek at me through the
ethnographic tint
Of eyeglasses?
And when shall you, O Light of the World!
Shine over the darkness that drapes
Like a black cloth over this wobbling,
Broken-legged table

Here, where soccer glory, like a tapestry,
Conceals my part of the fouled wall

Down, O deputies! you've let me
So down I can't see that horizon in which
The sun of hope rises
Against this sky tainted with drab despair

So into an iron bucket I lament, filling it with sighs
Force the content down your throat
So you know how acidofelous
Tastes the fruit of disillusionment; how briny
Smacks the mesocarpe of angst

For beastly the Times of tyranny have been
And this pain and blood I have to show
From the paw gashes
Of snarling decades that have pounced at me;

The fanged noons and the wolf-eyed dusks
Of ravening days that prowl these wilds of years

X
No defence counsel for the lowly arraigned
In this court of last instance
Under the ministry
Of neurosis and keeper of the sins
Of they who reduced – to a chameleon status –
The law of the land

And they've belittled me, O! Father in Heaven,
Down to a mere ruminant for slaughter;
Goat that chews the cud of days bitter than quinine

Then I listened between the lines
Of speeches addressed to their fellow quislings, hailing:
Long live the prawn
And us, clique of lice –dependent residents –
In this dandruffed hair of paupers.

XI
The sooth of chimney minds
Blackens immaculate prayers lisped like sighs
From the mouths of lip service, paid
To Him who carried on His head
A world full of sins

And praises to the Most High: they bounce off Him
And divert to the serpent for having been chorused
Out of the mouths of the sanctimonious-hearted,
How then can you change the world, O candidate

Of rotted innards in a stomach
Full of promises
That gas*ify* into a foetid flatulence?

And when they came; these saurian men
To where the road branched out
Into one ethereal path to take
And an earthly choice to make,
They all went the way of the wealth paved with dollar
bills

Reason why – mugfuls
Of paradisal bliss liquefied –
I drink in endless daydreams
Just to slake me
Of this Erebian thirst
From the flaming woe
That infernal*izes* the world

XII
TO SAVE A DYING PRAWN

In a far, light-years corner
Of enlightened thoughts farther than the ninth planet,
I voyage for the truth, lost
Before the birth
Of the brain which bore the ink
In those pens that have made us
Failed poets of men

And if you swallow inadvertently
That poison put into the food for the soul,
What better emetic to take, O! brother,

Than a look at the big picture of things which lie
Beyond that smile on the face of the self?
So in this hustle of the bustle; this struggle
Of nothingness in a toggle,
One thing only commands my tussle:
That no hand washes its own self but the other,
That no face is seen by its own eyes
But those of another

For when the great liar called life
Speaks ill of us through its mirror of five senses
Our stolen faces, so comely
Come back to us only as a gift, parcelled
In the foils of simulacra

XIII

Looking
For that last hope, lost
In this maze of numberless pilfering fingers,
Let us drink
From crying eyes that shed not tears
But admonishings
Of salvation for us; maggoty souls
Of this entire clan under water
And if we all take a plunge, brethren! into this river
Drowning in the waters that rise
From the mountains of Ecclesiastes,
It will be
To save a dying prawn

So in freedom's name
May we walk, O compatriots!
To that paradisal destination
Not on the stormy, mountainous road of devil's

advocates, quaking
With thunder and lightening, but on paths
Just thornier than wild roses

And let not smoking muzzles, carried
In guerrilla hands, be the goad
That moves us up to saner heights
But the prod of deep reason, felt
Like the stillness
Of lakes unperturbed